MW00886185

Essential Viewpoints

U.S. Sanctions on Cuba

Essential Viewpoints

U.S. Sanctions on Cuba

BY MARTIN GITLIN

Content Consultant
Sarah Stephens, Executive Director
Center for Democracy in the Americas

ABDO
Publishing Company

CREDITS

Published by ABDO Publishing Company, 8000 West 78th Street, Edina, Minnesota 55439.

Printed in the United States of America,
North Mankato, Minnesota
052010
092010

THIS BOOK CONTAINS AT LEAST 10% RECYCLED MATERIALS.

Editor: Melissa Johnson
Copy Editor: Rebecca Rowell
Interior Design and Production: Kazuko Collins
Cover Design: Kazuko Collins

Library of Congress Cataloging-in-Publication Data
Gitlin, Marty.
U.S. sanctions on Cuba / Martin Gitlin.
p. cm. — (Essential viewpoints)
Includes bibliographical references and index.
ISBN 978-1-61613-525-6
1. Economic sanctions, American—Cuba—Juvenile literature. 2. United States—Foreign economic relations—Cuba—Juvenile literature. 3. Cuba—Foreign economic relations—United States—Juvenile literature. I. Title.
HF1500.5.U5G58 2011
327.1'17—dc22

2010002657

TABLE OF CONTENTS

Chapter 1

The island of Cuba is located roughly 100 miles (161 km) south of Florida.

The Great Debate

In 2008, Fidel Castro, who had led the island nation of Cuba since 1959, stepped down permanently as the country's leader. Castro had led the Cuban Revolution in 1959 and helped his country reorganize with a communist economic system. In a communist system, the government controls the country's businesses and industries. In a capitalist system, such as the United States practices, individual people control business and industry. In communist Cuba, one political party has controlled the government since 1959. In the democratic United States, the people vote to decide who runs the government. The United States believes that democracy and capitalism are better than communism. Cuba believes the opposite. Both countries work to protect their own economic systems. At times, the United States has viewed communism as a threat to U.S. democracy. These differences of ideology have been at the root of the poor relationship between the United States and Cuba since the Cuban Revolution.

In Castro's message to the Cuban people as he stepped down, he said, "The path will always be difficult . . . The adversary to be defeated is extremely strong; however, we have been able to keep it at bay for half a century."[1] The adversary to whom Castro referred was the United States.

Cuba's Islands

The capital city of Havana and much of the rest of Cuba rests on its main island, but the entire country consists of more than 1,600 much smaller islands. The main island of Cuba runs 710 miles (1,150 km) long and is the sixteenth largest island in the world.

Fidel Castro was the leader of Cuba from 1959 to 2008.

Castro had been in poor health for several years. He had given temporary control of the government to his brother, Raúl Castro, in 2006. When Fidel left office in 2008, Raúl became Cuba's new leader. Many people wondered if there would be changes in Cuba under Raúl.

It quickly became clear that communism and one-party rule would remain in force under Raúl and that there would be no immediate, drastic change. Raúl proclaimed:

> *Fidel is irreplaceable and the people shall continue his work when he is no longer physically with us; [his ideas] have made it possible to build the beacon of dignity and justice our country represents. The Communist Party, a sure guarantee of the unity of the Cuban nation, is the sole worthy heir to our people's confidence in its leader.*[2]

U.S. Sanctions on Cuba

Since 1960, the United States has maintained a series of sanctions against Cuba. This means that the United States has refused to interact with Cuba in an attempt to make the country change how it is run. At different times, these sanctions have included bans on travel between the United States and Cuba and bans on trade between the countries. A primary reason for the sanctions has been to try to stop the spread of communism. The United States has also imposed sanctions to protest a lack of freedom and human rights in Cuba. Cuban citizens are denied freedom of speech and the press and the freedom to assemble in groups. Some are jailed without a trial. Many people believe that Fidel Castro and the Communist Party in Cuba have repressed political dissidents in order to remain in power.

The U.S. government has hoped that sanctions against Cuba would force the country to adopt democracy and a capitalist economic system, but those changes have not taken place. Even with Cuba's new leader, the country has continued to refuse to comply with U.S. conditions for lifting the sanctions.

Conflicted Opinion

As the situation in Cuba has shifted, many people who have supported one side of the argument have switched to the other side. One who has changed his mind is world political commentator and Latin American expert Alvaro Vargas Llosa. He said in April 2009:

> *I have been conflicted on this issue. . . . Until not long ago, I favored the embargo [sanctions]. As an advocate of free trade, I would normally have called such a measure an unacceptable restriction on the freedom of people to trade with whomever they pleased. But I thought that trading with a regime that had killed, jailed, exiled or muzzled countless of its citizens for decades was not a worthy objective, as it would also preserve that dictatorship.*
>
> *. . . Eventually, I admitted to myself that there was an intolerable inconsistency in my thinking. No democracy based on liberty should tell its citizens what country to visit or whom to trade with, regardless of the government under which they live. Even though the Castro brothers, Fidel and Raúl, would obtain a political victory in the very short run, the embargo could no longer be justified.*[3]

The Controversy

The sanctions are controversial. People on both sides of the debate dispute their potential to be effective, and opponents question whether the U.S. policy is morally right. The sanctions were imposed in order to force the leaders of Cuba to change their ways. Observers have argued, however, that sanctions have hurt the people much more than their leaders.

According to policy experts, the United States can take three possible actions regarding the restrictions. Each has possible benefits and problems, and people disagree about which approach is the best:

- The United States can maintain a hard-line approach. It can pressure the Cuban government by keeping full sanctions.

- The United States can soften the sanctions that most hurt Cubans while keeping some pressure on the Cuban government. It also could begin negotiations with the Cubans.

- The United States can end the sanctions immediately with no changes from Cuba.

One aspect of the debate has centered on whether sanctions work. The United States has hoped that outside pressure would restore democracy to Cuba. People in favor of the sanctions believe that taking away Cuba's trade will force the country to adopt a more democratic and capitalist system. They believe that backing down on the sanctions would only strengthen the Cuban communist regime.

Many Cuban people live in poverty. Both sides of the debate argue how much of the poverty is due to U.S. sanctions and how much is due to the Cuban government and its communist system. People against the sanctions argue that increasing the Cuban people's contact with the outside world will expose them to capitalism and democracy. More exposure to these ideas might inspire them to change their own country.

The debate has also focused on the legitimacy of the U.S. policy. Should the United States decide what is best for the Cuban people? Is it right to intervene in other countries in order to stop communism or human rights abuses? Is there evidence that the sanctions will eventually work?

"Concessions to the dictatorship [including ending the sanctions] embolden it to further isolate, imprison and brutalize pro-democracy activists, to continue to dictate which Cubans and Cuban-Americans are able to enter the island, and [provide] the dictatorship with critical financial support."[4]

—U.S. Representatives Lincoln Diaz-Balart and Mario Diaz-Balart of Florida speaking against loosening the sanctions on Cuba, April 13, 2009

Poverty is widespread in Cuba.

Chapter 2

Christopher Columbus landed in Cuba in 1492.

Early History

Several weeks after Christopher Columbus set sail from Spain in 1492, he set his eyes upon a beautiful sight. He saw the coast of Cuba. According to legend, he deemed it "the loveliest land ever beheld by human eyes."[1]

Soon, hundreds of Spanish explorers began arriving on the island to organize settlements. The native population was often mistreated, forced into slavery, or killed by the settlers. Cuba eventually became a Spanish colony.

The people of Cuba would not be free from foreign control for centuries. Great Britain staged a military takeover in 1762. The following year, it returned Cuba to Spain in exchange for Florida.

The Cubans, however, continued to press for their independence. A large conflict beginning in 1868 resulted in thousands of deaths. It also led the Spanish government to promise to end slavery and institute reforms such as freedom of speech and assembly. However, those promises were never kept. Slavery finally ended in 1886, but it would take a war and a major decision by the United States for Cubans to become self-governing.

Leading the fight for liberation was Cuban poet and teacher Jose Marti, who led a rebellion in 1895.

Slavery

Slavery was legal in the United States before Congress passed the Thirteenth Amendment in 1865. In the United States, slaves were primarily black people who had been kidnapped from Africa; their descendants were born into slavery. The same was true in Cuba. But after slavery was abolished there in 1886, the Spanish who controlled the country brought in a large number of Chinese to work on tobacco and sugar plantations. The Chinese laborers suffered just as black slaves of previous generations had.

His death at the hands of the Spanish royalist army that year angered his countrymen, who declared Cuba free that summer. The Spanish refused to recognize Cuban independence, but the revolutionaries continued to fight. In April 1898, the United States became involved out of self-interest. U.S. leaders wanted European powers such as Spain to have less influence in the Western Hemisphere, and so they backed Cuban rebel forces. The resulting conflict became known as the Spanish-American War.

Four months later, Spain surrendered and soon gave power over Cuba, Puerto Rico, and its possessions in the Philippines and the West Indies to the United States. The United States ruled Cuba for four years before granting it independence in 1902. But as part of the deal, the Cubans were forced to accept the Platt Amendment. This agreement gave the United States broad power to intervene in situations in which

Maine Explosion

The Spanish-American War began after a U.S. ship, the *Maine*, exploded and sank in a harbor off the Cuban coast. At the time, the United States blamed the incident on a Spanish attack. Further investigations have indicated that the explosion might have been the result of a coal fire onboard, but no one knows for sure why the ship sank. The United States might have used media reports that Spain was to blame as an excuse to join the fight against Spanish control of Cuba.

The sinking of the USS Maine *in Cuba helped spark U.S. involvement in the Spanish-American War.*

Cuban independence was threatened from forces both inside and outside the country. The Platt Amendment was repealed in 1934.

Cuban Dictators

Many Cubans resented the U.S. presence in their country. The United States influenced elections and manipulated the economy, investing millions of dollars in businesses on the island by the early

1920s. The United States controlled large parts of the sugar industry, which provided Cuba its greatest revenue. But most Cubans were not benefiting from U.S. investments. Poverty and unemployment were still widespread, particularly during the Great Depression of the 1930s.

As a result, worker strikes and revolutionary protests increased. General Gerardo Machado y Morales was elected president of Cuba in 1924. This was greatly due to the backing of U.S. investors who believed he would reward them for their support.

Machado proved to be a corrupt and ruthless dictator who had political opponents tortured and murdered. A group led by Fulgencio Batista overthrew him in 1933. Batista then appointed himself military chief and named Ramón Grau San Martín president. Batista continued to rule behind the scenes, however, and was elected to office himself in 1940.

A year later, Cuba joined the United States and its allies in helping secure victory in World War II. But after the conflict, life was not much better for the Cuban people. Though a new constitution allowed all Cubans to vote and provided improved conditions for workers, the government remained corrupt. And the United States, whose businesses continued to benefit financially from Cuban workers and imports, took no action.

Grau regained the presidency in 1944, followed by Carlos Prío Socarrás in 1948. When it was clear he would not win with votes, Batista again took office in 1952 through a military coup. He went on to brutalize those he feared threatened his power.

Failed Revolution

Many Cubans became unhappy with the status quo, including brothers Fidel and Raúl Castro. They decided to honor the centennial of the birth of their hero, Jose Marti, in the summer of 1953. They did so by staging an uprising at the Moncada army barracks in the town of Santiago de Cuba on July 26. But the attack failed. The brothers, as well as their fellow revolutionaries, were arrested.

Castro's Speech

Fidel Castro made his most famous speech during his trial after being arrested in 1953. It was titled "History Will Absolve Me." During the speech, he spoke about the Cubans for whom he was fighting: "When we speak of the people we are not talking about those who . . . welcome any repressive regime, any dictatorship, any despotism. . . . When we speak of struggle and we mention the people we mean the vast unredeemed masses, those to whom everyone makes promises and who are deceived by all; we mean the people who yearn for a better, more dignified and more just nation."[2]

Raúl Castro with Che Guevara during the Cuban Revolution

Fidel Castro was certainly not repentant at his trial. He criticized the government and the policies he believed caused the nation's widespread poverty. He spent the next two years in prison. Upon Castro's release in May 1955, Batista forced him and his brother to leave Cuba.

Batista would regret not dealing with the Castros more harshly. The brothers and their followers traveled to Mexico, where they began plotting an armed rebellion in Cuba. They planned the revolt alongside Argentinean Ernesto "Che" Guevara, who shared their revolutionary beliefs and spirit.

The Castros, Guevara, and approximately 80 rebels returned to Cuba in December 1956. They lived in hiding while attempting to gain support, mainly from students and others under 30 years of age. In March 1957, the brothers and their followers attacked the Presidential Palace in Havana. They tried to kill Batista and take over the radio system to proclaim the revolution a success.

The Legend of Che Guevara

Although Fidel Castro would assume control of Cuba in 1959, no one embodied the spirit of the revolution more than Che Guevara. Born in Argentina in 1928, Guevara became interested in politics as a child by reading books in his father's library. He read the works of nineteenth-century German philosopher Karl Marx, who has been credited with the founding of communism.

During Guevara's years studying medicine at the University of Buenos Aires, he journeyed the length of South America on a motorcycle. He was touched by the terrible conditions faced by many of its poorest people.

In 1954, Guevara moved to Mexico, where he eventually met Fidel Castro. They began to plan the overthrow of the Cuban government. Following the revolution, Guevara was appointed by Castro as the president of Cuba's national bank and eventually minister for industry in 1961. He also served as an ambassador for Cuba around the world and attempted to start rebellions in Latin America and Africa.

Guevara became a hero to revolutionary thinkers around the globe. These included many U.S. college students who had become disillusioned with their government and its policies in the 1960s. Guevara was killed by Bolivian security forces during a trip to create unrest among peasants and workers there in 1967.

The plot failed, but the rebels did seize weapons from an army garrison for future operations. They became more open in their fight to overthrow the government. Castro's followers set fire to sugarcane fields to prevent the Batista government and foreign businesses from profiting from them. The revolutionaries began battling soldiers in the streets and luring more Cuban peasants and students into their ranks.

The spirit of revolution became so strong in Cuba that Batista was forced to flee to Spain on New Year's Eve, 1958. Castro and his band of revolutionaries had triumphed. They marched into Havana on January 2, 1959, and proclaimed a new government.

Cuban dictator Fulgencio Batista was overthrown by Fidel Castro in 1959.

Chapter 3

Castro and the Soviets, led by Nikita Khrushchev, right, were on friendly terms.

Cold War History

Much of the conflict between the United States and Cuba dates back to a period of history known as the Cold War, which developed after World War II (1939–1945). As World War II ended, the United States and the Soviet Union became the strongest and most influential nations on earth. The Soviet Union's communist system was seen as opposite of—and hostile to—the capitalist system of the United States. Communism is based on government control of goods and production, while capitalism relies on free markets. The two systems have competing ideas about personal freedom and the role of government.

The Soviet Union gained control of Eastern Europe after World War II. Meanwhile, the U.S. government, which had always considered communism a threat to the American way of life, backed the democratic nations of Western Europe.

Communism Spreads

The U.S. government was alarmed when the Soviet Union and China began to spread the communist doctrine to other parts of the world. The United States sent troops to

The Domino Theory

During the Cold War, anticommunists believed in the domino theory. This theory maintained that if one country fell to communism, others in the same region would do the same. People who believed in this theory insisted that by fighting in Korea and Vietnam from the 1950s to the 1970s, the United States prevented communism from spreading to other parts of the world. This has been one argument for maintaining sanctions against Cuba.

Others assert that this theory has not held up, using Asia as an example. In Asia, communist expansion has not occurred despite its decades-long presence in China, North Korea, and Vietnam. Also, Cuba has been a communist country for several decades, and it remains the only one in the Western Hemisphere.

fight wars in Korea and, later, Vietnam to prevent communism from taking over in those Asian countries.

Communist revolutionaries around the world pushed for the doctrine's spread. Among them was Fidel Castro. The United States had to decide how to react to Castro's takeover in 1959. Some felt the U.S. government should establish normal diplomatic relations with Cuba. They argued that Cuba would not necessarily be an enemy of the United States simply because the countries followed different political and economic philosophies.

Others disagreed, arguing that the creation of the first communist government in the Western Hemisphere would be a threat to the United States. They further argued that the United States should always fight communism—if not with weapons, then through economic and political pressure—particularly so close to home. Some worried that the Soviet Union could place military bases in Cuba from which they could launch an invasion of the United States.

Cuban Exiles

In the three years after the Cuban Revolution of 1959, nearly 200,000 people left the country. Emigrants included many anticommunists who left for political reasons. Others who left belonged to higher economic classes. They feared that their wealth would be taken from them under a communist system.

Castro met U.S. Vice President Nixon, right*, in 1959.*

Castro's First Moves

When Fidel Castro installed the new government in 1959, he offered friendship to the United States. In April, Castro traveled to Washington DC to meet with Vice President Richard Nixon. The United States and U.S. President Dwight Eisenhower had already officially recognized the new Cuban government. But U.S. officials soon grew alarmed by reports that their island neighbor was becoming a communist state. U.S.-Cuban relations did not start as well as they could have when Nixon and Castro met, according to Castro biographer Carlos Franqui.

> *The meeting between Fidel and Nixon was an out-and-out disaster; their mutual dislike would be long-lived. Fidel's strategy was to seem a friend to all; he would offer his hand and let the others not shake it. And in Washington the prevailing atmosphere was pure disdain.*[1]

Cuban Cigars

Cigar smokers were one group of Americans affected by the 1962 U.S. trade embargo against Cuba. Cuba is known for making some of the finest cigars in the world. Many are painstakingly hand-rolled by skilled factory workers, who generally make approximately 100 cigars a day. The country exported more than 125 million cigars in 1998. In the United States, however, the selling or purchasing of Cuban cigars remains illegal.

That ill will grew. Castro hoped that the United States would offer aid to his country without insisting on the right to influence Cuba's political and economic future. But when it became apparent that Castro had no intention of maintaining a democracy and a capitalist economy in Cuba, his relationship with the United States soured.

Tensions grew in 1960 when Castro ordered that his new government take over all property in Cuba owned by foreign corporations. Much of that property included banks, oil refineries, and sugar industries owned by U.S. citizens. The result was a $2 billion loss for U.S. businesses—a loss Cuba refused to pay back. By October 19, the United States struck back by forbidding U.S. exports to Cuba other than food and medical supplies.

Early reports on Castro's human rights record were another factor in the deteriorating relationship between Cuba and the United States. He put on trial 500 political opponents who had played roles in the Batista government. Then he broadcast their gruesome execution by firing squad to the Cuban public. When U.S. officials protested, Castro boasted, "If the Americans don't like what's happening in Cuba, they can land the Marines and then there will be 200,000 [Americans] dead."[2]

The Bay of Pigs Disaster

No U.S. forces were on the way to Cuba. But the U.S. Central Intelligence Agency (CIA) was busy training approximately 1,400 Cuban exiles for an attack it hoped would bring down Castro's new regime. The operation at the Bay of Pigs, located on Cuba's southern shore, began on April 17, 1961, shortly after John F. Kennedy became the U.S.

President Kennedy addressed the nation during the Cuban Missile Crisis.

president. The invasion fell apart quickly as Cuban forces sank two of the Cuban exiles' ships and shot down several airplanes. The operation ended within days.

The Bay of Pigs event, as well as Castro's actions and remarks, destroyed any chance at normal diplomatic relations with the United States. The superpower announced that it was cutting off all trade with Cuba. Several thousand miles away, the leaders of the communist Soviet Union saw an opportunity. They decided that making friends with a revolutionary such as Castro and a country so near the shores of the United States could prove beneficial.

The Soviet Union began providing Cuba with economic assistance and became an eager trading partner. In the summer of 1962, the Soviet Union placed nuclear missiles in Cuba that were capable of reaching the United States. Castro claimed that the United States was plotting to overthrow his government. In his view, accepting the missiles was a necessary defensive strategy.

On October 14, 1962, a U.S. intelligence airplane photographed the Soviet missile silos in Cuba. The finding was reported to President Kennedy on October 16.

The Cuban Missile Crisis

In the tense 13 days that followed, the world came as close to a nuclear war as it ever has, according to historians. President Kennedy and his advisors discussed various responses, which included an air strike against the missile bases. That plan was discarded in favor of a naval blockade in Cuban waters. The idea was to stop any incoming shipments of missiles or related equipment.

President Kennedy feared that such a step might still lead to a nuclear exchange that could cause millions of deaths. He informed the nation about the crisis in an address on national television. Frightened people across the country held their breath as President Kennedy ordered Soviet leader Nikita Khrushchev to remove the missiles.

Those same people let out sighs of relief when

"Pedro Pan" Children

After Castro assumed control, many Cubans wanted their children to grow up in a democracy. Some parents feared their children would be sent to the Soviet Union or the mountains of Cuba as part of Castro's special training program. Others believed the move to communism would prevent their children from being given a Catholic education. These parents worked in secret to have their children sent to the United States through an effort called "Operation Pedro Pan."

The secret mission was authorized by the U.S. government and undertaken by the Catholic Welfare Bureau. The group originally agreed to help bring approximately 200 Cuban children to the United States. But from December 1960 to October 1962, more than 14,000 youngsters were airlifted from Cuba to the country. Approximately 150,000 relatives of "Pedro Pan" children eventually joined them in the United States, although many more were never reunited with their family members.

Among the children sent away from parents in Cuba was Antonio Garcia, who later worked as a car washer in Miami, Florida. "Overall, it was a good thing because it saved us from communism," said Garcia in a 1998 interview. "But I have told my mother, and I know it pains her, that I would never do to my own children, if I had them, what my parents did to me."[3]

Khrushchev agreed to the U.S. terms on October 28. In return, President Kennedy had to promise not to invade Cuba and to remove U.S. missiles from Turkey—a small price to pay for peace.

Castro the Communist

By the time of the Cuban Missile Crisis, Castro had announced that he would pattern his government and economy after those of the Soviet Union. He spoke freely about a society in which Cubans were motivated more by helping their fellow citizens than by earning a lot of money. He built schools and hospitals and helped people become doctors and other medical professionals. He wanted to provide the necessities of life for every Cuban. But in the meantime, he placed the media and schools under government control and ended freedom of speech and assembly. He appointed judges who punished those he believed were political enemies.

Although such trends in Cuba disturbed U.S. leaders, they had more pressing issues to face during the turbulent 1960s and 1970s. The United States was involved in a war in Vietnam that was becoming increasingly unpopular. President Kennedy was assassinated in November 1963. Robert Kennedy, the president's brother, was killed while campaigning for the presidency in 1968. Civil rights leader Martin Luther King Jr. was also murdered that year. In addition, African Americans, angered by discrimination, rioted in cities throughout the country. And the Watergate scandal forced President Richard Nixon to resign in 1974, which heightened public cynicism about the U.S. government.

Castro remained in power throughout these decades. In 1980, he made a sweeping move to rid Cuba of those who wished to leave in what became known as the Mariel Boatlift. For six months during the spring and summer, Castro invited anyone who was unhappy in Cuba to leave. Cubans packed boats and flooded into Florida. An estimated 125,000 completed the journey.

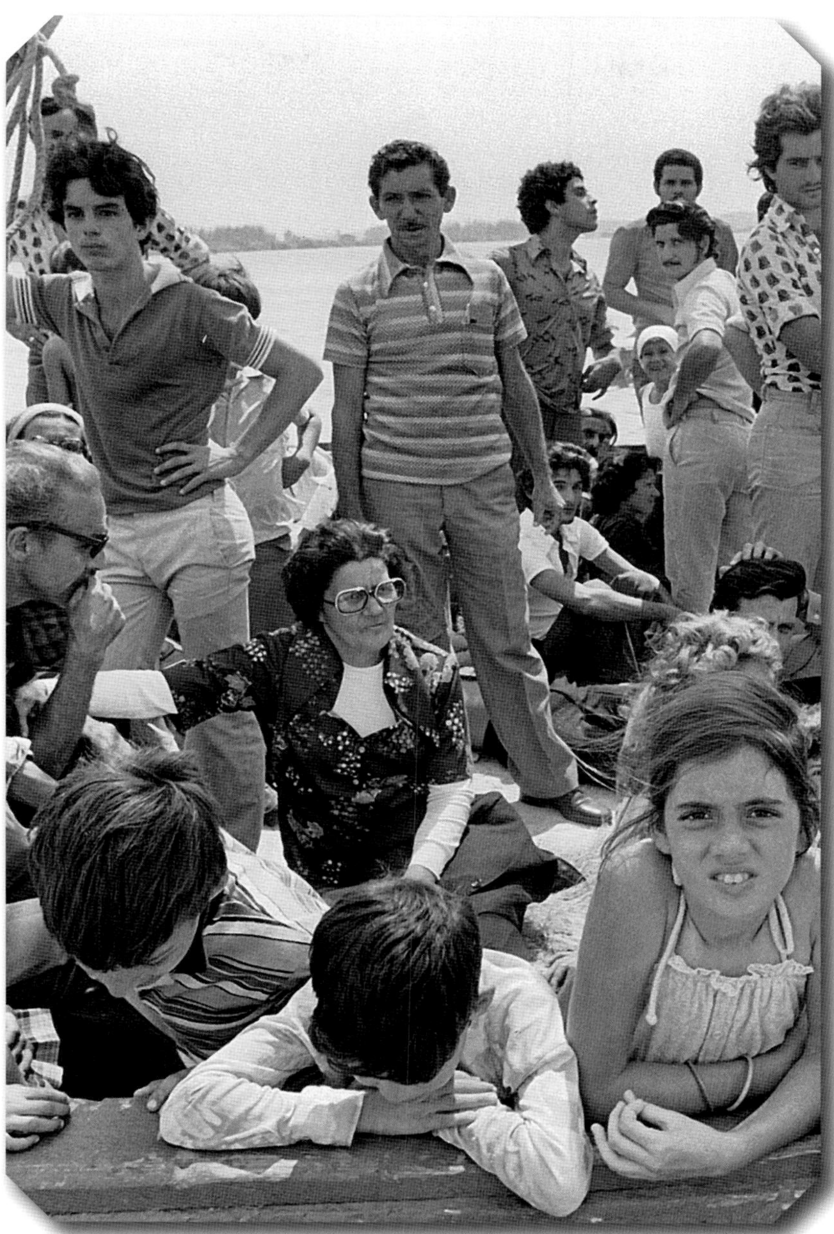

Thousands of Cubans left the country during the Mariel Boatlift.

Chapter 4

Cubans wait in a food line. Citizens of the communist nation have often faced shortages of basic necessities.

Recent History

Changes in Eastern Europe in the late 1980s and early 1990s led to changes in Cuba. Because of a failing economy and increasing calls for individual freedoms from its citizens, the Soviet Union began employing a more free-market capitalist system. Ultimately, the Soviet Union broke apart in 1991.

The Soviet Union cut its economic support to Cuba in 1989, which proved devastating for the island nation. During what became known in Cuba as the Special Period, industry and production were cut back dramatically. But Castro insisted on maintaining a communist system despite the hardships experienced by his people.

Without assistance from the Soviet Union, Cuba experienced a huge drop in its gross domestic product, which is a basic measure of an economy's performance. It fell 35 percent from 1989 to 1993. Shortages of food and fuel increased, and living conditions worsened. A serious housing shortage forced many families to live in cramped apartments. At this time, Cuban immigration to the United States peaked because of the economic situation. Unlimited numbers of Cuban refugees had been allowed to enter the United States before this time. The huge wave of immigrants prompted the U.S. government to change its policy. In 1994, it allowed only 20,000 Cubans legal entrance to the country each year.

Enter the Dollar

In 1993, Cuba legalized the possession and use of the U.S. dollar, which became the nation's most desired currency. In state-run "dollar stores," Cubans with U.S. dollars could buy hard-to-find items such as imported foods, clothing, and modern electronic games and devices.

But the acceptance of U.S. currency widened the economic differences among Cubans. Those with dollars improved their lives, while those without suffered. Some Cubans had dollars sent to them by their relatives in the United States. Cubans who worked with tourists—such as waiters, taxi drivers, and bartenders—received dollars, which were far more valuable than the Cuban peso. Often, doctors, teachers, and government officials worked second jobs to serve foreign tourists. In this way, they earned valuable U.S. dollars.

During this time, the Cuban government took a number of other

Cuban Immigrants

The huge influx of Cuban immigrants arriving on U.S. shores motivated the two countries to work out an agreement in 1994. In that year, the United States set a quota of 20,000 visas allotted to Cubans annually. That number represents only 4 percent of Cubans who seek residency in the United States—approximately 500,000 Cubans apply for visas every year. And some Cubans whose applications are not accepted attempt to emigrate illegally. Others do so because they cannot afford to emigrate legally. The combined cost of a permit, passport, necessary medical check-up, and plane fare was more than $1,000 in 2010.

small steps toward capitalism. In 1993, Cubans were permitted to be self-employed in certain occupations. This meant that they could make money independently. New markets were opened for farmers and artisans in 1994, so they could profit from what they produced. Individuals were allowed to open restaurants and catering businesses for themselves in 1995.

That same year, the Cuban government opened the country to foreign investment. The majority of foreign investors had been removed from the country shortly after the Cuban Revolution. The government tightly regulated the little foreign investment it allowed. After the changes in 1995, foreign investors were once again allowed to invest in or own businesses in Cuba in nearly every industry.

Changing Sanctions

Though U.S. sanctions against Cuba have remained fairly constant for nearly 50 years, they have undergone a number of minor changes. Often, these revisions have been connected to the current politics and U.S. sentiments about communism.

In 1982, President Ronald Reagan banned travel to and business with the island nation. He believed

Cuba was encouraging unrest and pushing for communism in Latin America.

The United States tightened its economic policy against Cuba in 1992 by enacting the Cuban Democracy Act. It barred foreign-based U.S. companies from trading with Cuba and prevented countries that traded with the United States from doing the same with Cuba. Countries that disregarded the act could lose the right to trade with the United States.

Sending Cash Home

Cash sent from Americans to Cubans has formed a large part of the Cuban economy for many years. In 2004, the Commission for Assistance to a Free Cuba estimated that Americans sent between $400 million and $800 million each year to Cuban family members. Since the dollar ban went into effect in 2004, 10 percent of this money has gone directly to the Cuban government.

President Bill Clinton eased restrictions on travel in 1995. Then, on February 24, 1996, the Cuban air force shot down two U.S. civilian planes flying near the island nation. These planes were flown by Cuban-American pilots representing Brothers to the Rescue, a Miami-based group that searches the sea for refugees. Clinton and other U.S. leaders responded by creating the Helms-Burton Act in 1996. This act further tightened sanctions on businesses and groups that traded with the United States and Cuba.

In 1998 and 1999, relations eased once more as President Clinton again allowed Americans to fly directly to Cuba and to send money to Cuban relatives. In 2000, an act of Congress allowed Americans once again to sell crops and food to Cubans, with some restrictions. In 2002, President George W. Bush announced humanitarian aid and suggested restoring direct mail service to Cuba. He hoped that doing so would motivate Cubans to push their government for reform. However, as of 2010, direct mail service from the United States to Cuba had yet to be restored and

The Elián González Story

On Thanksgiving Day in 1999, five-year-old Cuban Elián González was found floating on a life raft off the coast of Florida. He was one of three survivors in a group of 13 who had set out on a small boat for Miami. The other ten, including his mother and her boyfriend, had drowned.

A spirited debate began when both the Cuban government and Elián's father, Juan Miguel González, insisted that his boy be returned to his native country. Some argued that Castro would make Elián's life miserable if he were sent back. Others asserted that Elián's father—his remaining parent—had every right to have his son returned.

An estimated 50,000 Cubans showed up in Havana in a government-sponsored march to demand that Elián be sent back. And in late March 2000, a U.S. federal judge ruled that the boy be returned to Cuba.

Since his Miami, Florida, relatives refused to give him back, federal agents stormed into their home to take Elián away and reunite him with his father. Soon, Elián and his father were on a plane back to Cuba, but Elián was certainly not forgotten in the United States.

President Clinton addressed reporters after Cuba shot down two U.S. aircraft in 1996.

diplomatic talks continued. By 2002, Cuba was importing more crops and food from the United States than from any other country.

Relations Turn Chilly

President Bush generally pushed for more strict enforcement of sanctions during his time in office. He tightened the restrictions on travel in 2004 and made it more difficult to sell food and crops to Cubans. The U.S. government also began a closer watch on foreign banks, cracking down on those that exchanged U.S. dollars with the Cuban government.

As the Cuban economy recovered from the Special Period, Castro began to roll back other economic reforms. He began tightening government control in many areas that he had previously loosened. Stricter rules for small businesses forced many to close. In 2004, in response to tighter U.S. sanctions, Castro ended the use of the U.S. dollar in Cuba. Dollars became unacceptable as currency in Cuban stores. Instead, people had to convert U.S. dollars into a currency called convertible pesos, which were usable only on the island. The Cuban government began to charge a 10 percent conversion fee, making it more difficult for Cubans in the United States to send money home to their relatives.

Helms-Burton Act

In addition to tightening the sanctions on Cuba, the Helms-Burton Act took away some power from the U.S. president. According to this law, the president cannot remove the sanctions on Cuba until either Congress agrees or until Cuba meets specific targets for democracy.

With the introduction of convertible pesos, the country created a system of two competing currencies. Cubans still earned pesos from their government jobs. They could earn convertible pesos by the same means that they once earned dollars.

Pesos are not worth very much, so Cubans need convertible pesos if they want the kinds of imported goods that they once bought in dollar stores. Lately, other currencies, such as Euros, Canadian dollars, and Japanese yen, have become more widely circulated in Cuba in place of U.S. dollars.

Big Changes

On July 31, 2006, an aging and ailing Fidel Castro handed over temporary leadership of Cuba to his brother Raúl. On February 19, 2008, Castro stepped down for good. After gaining permanent control of the country, Raúl indicated he would be open to improving relations with the United States.

President Barack Obama initiated the most sweeping sanction reforms in 2009. His changes made it easier for Cuban Americans to visit their relatives. The changes also increased the amount of money Americans could send to relatives in Cuba annually and lifted travel restrictions on U.S. businesspeople selling food and medicine to Cuba. These changes might represent the first step toward improved diplomatic relations.

Many people believe that Cuba will not change under its new leader, Raúl Castro.

Chapter 5

Cuban Americans rally in support of U.S. sanctions.

The Policy of Sanctions

The United States has enforced various sanctions on Cuba since 1960, and in 2009, bans on both travel and trade were in effect. The Office of Foreign Assets Control (OFAC), run by the U.S. Treasury Department, has strictly enforced the U.S. policy. These sanctions have affected people and businesses in both Cuba and the United States in a number of ways.

The Scope of Sanctions

Under U.S. sanctions as of 2010, travel to Cuba by U.S. residents was extremely limited. The intent of the travel ban was to prevent Americans from helping the Cuban economy. However, Cuba welcomed millions of tourists from many other countries.

Certain groups of Americans were allowed to travel to Cuba with a general license, which did not require special permission from the OFAC. Among those eligible for the license were Cuban Americans who would reunite with family rather than spend money on a vacation. Professionals in various lines of work were permitted to visit Cuba as well.

In order to limit large sums of money from passing between the two nations, both U.S. travelers to Cuba and Cuban travelers to the United

Penalties

U.S. sanctions on Cuba apply to U.S. corporations and all U.S. citizens and permanent residents, even if they are living abroad. Violations of such sanctions against Cuba range from jail time of up to ten years to fines of $250,000 for individuals and $1 million for corporations.

U.S. citizens are not allowed to bring Cuban goods into the United States, including souvenirs.

States could carry no more than $3,000 into the country they were visiting. Americans could also send $1,000 to a Cuban planning on immigrating to the United States. Once that individual had received his or her visa from the U.S. State Department, he or she could receive an additional $1,000.

In 2010, the United States also enforced a trade embargo on Cuba. This meant that it was illegal to sell most U.S. goods and services in Cuba or to Cuban people. Exceptions included some publications and educational materials, some services related to telephones and the Internet, and some types of medicine and food. It was also illegal for U.S. citizens, residents, and companies to bring Cuban goods and services into the United States. It was illegal whether the goods were purchased in Cuba or in some other country. This strict ban even included small items such as souvenirs. Exceptions were made for some educational materials and some works of art. It was also illegal for U.S. banks to deal with Cuban banks. This meant that Americans could not use their debit or credit cards in Cuba.

Encouraging Change

The United States used a two-pronged approach to encourage political change in Cuba. The first part was the punitive sanctions. The second part, however, used positive measures to support Cubans who wanted political change in their country.

The United States encouraged nongovernmental humanitarian groups to provide aid to the Cuban people. Beginning in the 1980s, the United States provided funding for a radio and television station that broadcast democratic ideas to Cuba. The Cuban government jammed these signals, however, so that the broadcasts could not reach its citizens. The programs have also been criticized for having poor content. The United States also did what it could to aid dissidents and human rights activists in Cuba.

Who Can Travel to Cuba?

The United States has specific rules about who can travel to Cuba for business. Anyone wishing to travel to the island nation must apply for permission from the U.S. government. Among those permitted to visit Cuba are journalists on assignment. U.S.-based government officials, including those from foreign countries, are also allowed to do business in Cuba. Exceptions are also made for full-time academics, such as professors and researchers, and members of professional organizations.

A general license will also allow those who market, sell, or deliver agricultural products, medicine, or medical equipment to travel to Cuba. Employees of telecommunications services may also do business there.

Others must receive a specific license from the Office of Foreign Assets Control. These potential travelers are students, teachers, those involved in religious activities undertaken on the island, and people providing humanitarian efforts believed to be helping only the Cuban people, as opposed to the government. Performers such as musical entertainers and athletes may also be granted specific licenses to travel to Cuba.

Are Sanctions Effective?

U.S. policy in Cuba is not

unusual; the United States has imposed sanctions on a number of countries. Some sanctions have been more effective than others.

Throughout U.S. history, the government has stopped trade with enemy countries during times of war. For example, the United States halted trade with Vietnam during and following the Vietnam War (ca. 1959–1975). Trade relations with Vietnam were returned to normal in the 1990s.

Some sanctions have been effective. The United States joined other countries in prohibiting trade with South Africa in the mid-1980s to end apartheid, a system of laws that discriminated against nonwhites. It is generally believed that these international sanctions reinforced protests in the country that led to the end of apartheid in the mid-1990s.

However, sanctions do not always bring about the desired change. In 1997, a study by the Institute for International Economics revealed that sanctions enforced by the United States since 1970 achieved foreign policy goals less than 20 percent of the time. The study also claimed that sanctions cost the United States between $15 billion and $19 billion a year in lost revenue from exports.

An Ambassador's Opinion

Former Canadian ambassador Jeremy Kinsman wrote an opinion piece in the *New York Times* in April 2009. In it, he argued that Cuba was undergoing a slow transition toward democracy and that the sanctions had hurt the country. He thought that the Cuban people were unhappy, but they would not rise up against the government. He explained:

"In Havana Cubans appear exhausted from trying to make ends meet in a heavily bureaucratized run-around. They seem veiled by melancholy. Their anger at [U.S. President] Bush's [strengthened sanctions] vies with frustration over leaders who care more for ideology than public welfare.

"Still, the regime won't topple, as exiles hoped. Political opposition is marginalized. Cubans focus hopes on better living conditions."[2]

The United States and other countries imposed sanctions on Iraq in the 1990s to force the country's dictator, Saddam Hussein, to reduce his military. The sanctions denied basic necessities to the Iraqi people, while Hussein remained uncooperative and unaffected by the restrictions. Tens of thousands of Iraqi children died from diseases caused by lack of food and medicine, which some believe to be directly related to the U.S. policy. The sanctions remained in place until 2003, when Hussein was captured and removed from power during the U.S.-led invasion of Iraq.

"Sanctions have become a cheap way of doing foreign policy, except the costs are often really quite terrible," said John Mueller, a political scientist at the University of Rochester.[1] Mueller also argued that sanctions should be aimed at stopping technology used to make weapons and should not include food or medicine.

Despite sanctions, human rights and democracy are still lacking in such countries as Cuba, Iraq, and Iran. Sanctions and threats of sanctions also did not prevent Iran, North Korea, India, and Pakistan from researching or testing nuclear weapons.

How Do Sanctions Affect Cuba?

Cuba is relatively poor, and many modern goods have been unavailable to its residents. Even with food ration cards from the government, the average Cuban wage is too small to provide the basic necessities of life. Buildings have crumbled since the revolution, and new cars, technology, and other equipment are out of reach for most Cubans. Although health care is provided for free, medicine is difficult to obtain legally.

Getting around Cuba

One effect of the trade embargo against Cuba is a lack of automobiles in the country. Most Cubans do not own cars and are accustomed to using public transportation. Many Cubans also ride bicycles to travel short distances. The cars driven by Cubans are generally outdated U.S. models built before the 1959 revolution or models manufactured in the former Soviet Union. Cars with air conditioning are considered a luxury.

Many Cubans resort to buying food and other basic necessities illegally on the black market.

However, it is difficult to determine the true cause of Cuba's poverty. Life in Cuba grew worse after the country lost the support of the Soviet Union in 1989. Some people believe Cuba's economic troubles are caused by U.S. sanctions. They argue that sanctions should be lifted to improve the lives of Cuba's people. Others argue that the bad conditions in Cuba are caused by the communist system and Fidel Castro's leadership. They believe Cuba's economic situation will not improve until the island adopts capitalism.

Cuba's buildings are crumbling and its cars are old.

Chapter 6

The Castro brothers have controlled Cuba since 1959.

The Castros and Life in Cuba

No single person has had a greater impact on Cuban politics and U.S.-Cuba relations than Fidel Castro. Castro led the country from 1959 to 2008, during which time the United States had ten different presidents. Raúl described his brother during a speech commemorating the fiftieth anniversary of the Cuban Revolution:

> *We know that a man alone doesn't make history, but some men are indispensable as they can have a decisive influence in the course of events. Fidel is one of them; nobody doubts it, not even his most bitter enemies.*[1]

In 2010, although Fidel had officially retired from office, his opinions and persona still loomed large on the island. Many experts believed that no change could occur in Cuba as long as Fidel lived, even though he had stopped actively governing.

Some argue that lifting sanctions would allow the Cuban leaders to protect their pride while slowly instituting democracy and capitalism. The Castro brothers are not likely to admit that communism has failed their country. In fact, both have steadfastly maintained that both the economic system and their leadership have dramatically improved conditions in Cuba.

"Cubans of my generation either feel hatred or love for Fidel, or perhaps a mixture of both. We do not see him simply as a European or American head of state, questionable, sometimes ridiculous, and always exposed to criticism. He is the living legend of a revolutionary era. A solemn and heroic presence with an almost familiar, intensely affectionate relationship with the people."[2]

—Rafael Rojas, Cuban historian

Changing their course now, with sanctions in place, would mean admitting they were wrong. Lifting the sanctions would stop the attempt to make the Castros back down. This might allow gradual change to happen.

However, others argue that lifting the sanctions will reward the Castros and strengthen their regime. The United States has laid out specific steps that Cuba must take to lift the sanctions. These steps include allowing open elections and releasing political prisoners. Supporters of continuing the sanctions argue that

Fidel's Philosophy

Socially and economically, communism is supposed to be a humanitarian system. It is intended to distribute wealth so that everyone has the necessities of life. In a 1979 speech to the United Nations General Assembly, Fidel Castro spoke about his vision for the world:

> *There is often talk of human rights, but it is also necessary to talk of the rights of humanity. Why should some people walk barefoot so that others can travel in luxurious cars? Why should some live for 35 years, so that others can live for 70 years? Why should some be miserably poor, so that others can be hugely rich?*
>
> *I speak on behalf of the children of the world who do not have even a piece of bread. I speak on behalf of the sick who have no medicine, of those whose rights to life and human dignity have been denied. . . . What is the destiny of the latter? To starve to death? To be eternally poor?*[3]

Critics of Castro's point of view accept a greater gap between rich and poor in capitalist nations. Even with the gap, they argue, the overall standard of living in capitalist nations is much higher than it is in communist countries.

the United States must continue its current policy until Cuba gives in, or democracy will not be restored to the island.

Some Positive Aspects

Under Fidel's leadership, actions were taken that have improved the lives of the Cuban people. For many years, Fidel concentrated on improving science research, education, and health care on the island.

UNICEF is a United Nations organization that focuses on international child welfare. In 2007, according to that group, 97 percent of Cuba's children attended school, and 100 percent of its adults could read. These high numbers show that the Cuban commitment to education has had positive outcomes.

Cuba has government-run, universal health care, which means that all Cubans can visit doctors and

Cuban Medical Advances

Cuban medical products have been exported to dozens of other countries. U.S. companies have been particularly interested in the work of Cuban scientists researching cancer vaccines. Cuba has also developed the only vaccine to fight the disease meningitis B. GlaxoSmithKline, a U.S. drug company, considered the vaccine crucial. The company convinced the U.S. government to give it special permission to purchase the vaccine from Cuba.

Cuban researchers continue to have medical breakthroughs. In 2008, Cuban scientists announced the development of a vaccine that helps lung cancer patients live longer.

hospitals for free. On average, Cubans are as healthy and have as high a life expectancy as people in many developed countries who have higher individual incomes. This means that the Cuban health care system is able to maintain good health with fewer resources than many other countries. Cuba also has one of the best ratios of doctors to patients in the world.

Soon after Fidel Castro took power in 1959, he made the following announcement: "Cuba's future must, by necessity, be a future of scientists."[4] Cuba quickly established two scientific centers—an institute for research into sugarcane products and a national research center. By 1980, the country featured 35 scientific research centers at the university level—an increase of 29 centers since 1958. Thousands of science students were sent to communist countries in Eastern Europe to study as well.

Cuba's research centers have helped meet the nation's domestic needs and aided progress in developing countries around the world. In 1980, a visit from a U.S. cancer researcher inspired Castro to begin a national research program in biotechnology. The program has resulted in vaccines and other medications.

Cubans can also take pride in their cultural riches, including art, dance, music, and sports. There is a relatively even distribution of wealth in Cuba, which is the intended goal of the communist system. That has been accomplished despite the devastating loss of economic aid from the former Soviet Union. And Cuba's crime rate is far below the U.S. rate.

Poverty in Cuba

Despite the education and health care provided by the government, most of the Cuban people suffer from poverty. Low wages in all government-paid professions make it difficult for Cubans to pay for anything beyond the bare necessities rationed by the government. Many Cubans who do not have legal ways to make extra money or convertible pesos turn to the black market. They illegally buy the goods they need, such as clothing and medicine, and the goods they want, such as cell phones, refrigerators, and other foreign-made machines.

Cost of Living

Communism made several necessities more affordable to many Cubans. For example, utilities are almost free. In 2000, the average monthly electric bill for a typical family was approximately 15 pesos, which equals 66 U.S. cents. The monthly cost for water was about five pesos, or 13 U.S. cents.

Education in Cuba has greatly improved under the Castros.

During the 1980s, Cuba manufactured 80 percent of the medicine its people needed. However, after the fall of the Soviet Union in the 1990s and the loss of support from that superpower, Cuba could not acquire as many of the raw materials it needed to make medical products. There have been medical shortages ever since, and people have had trouble getting the medicine they need.

Cuba runs a system of food rationing, in which the government distributes food to the people to make sure no one starves. However, the amount of food is barely enough to live on. Many Cubans spend a significant percentage of their wages on extra food. In 2007, Associated Press reporter Anita Snow was based in Cuba and attempted to live one full month on the amount of food permitted by the rationing system. She lost nine pounds and wrote that during the experience, she found herself "obsessing about food."[5]

The Role of Sanctions

It has been estimated that in the 1990s alone, Cuba lost $70 billion in trade due to U.S. sanctions. Some argue that the financial hardships imposed by sanctions are a greater humanitarian threat than Cuba's repression. However, others argue that Cuba has fallen victim to the same economic problems suffered in Soviet-led countries because communism simply does not work.

Those who blame Cuba's poverty on the government note that the nation trades with the rest of the world. They believe that, with major trading partners in 2009 including Russia, China, and Venezuela, the government's poor handling of its economy has caused Cuba's poverty, not the U.S. sanctions. Others point to corruption within the

Cuban government, noting that Communist Party officials have access to luxuries denied to the rest of the Cuban people.

Others believe that sanctions imposed by the wealthiest country in the Western Hemisphere have caused great economic stress to the island. U.S. businesses and individual consumers purchase billions of dollars worth of goods and services every year. Lifting the trade embargo and travel restrictions would allow Cuba to improve its economy by exporting its goods and services to the United States and developing a thriving tourist industry.

The bottom line for those who oppose sanctions is that they do far more harm to the Cuban people than they do to Cuban leaders. While the loss of Soviet aid has greatly damaged the Cuban economy over the last two decades, the Castros and others in top government positions are isolated from the misery. Those who feel the United States should allow free trade with Cuba reason that doing so would better the lives of Cubans who desperately need help. After all, it is not the fault of the Cuban people that the Castros have been in charge, as the elections ensure that the Castros remain in power.

With the Castros in power, the Cuban people have not had the option to choose their leaders.

Chapter 7

The United States often sends troops or takes other actions in foreign countries.

The Right to Impose Sanctions

One important question in the issue of U.S. sanctions on Cuba is whether the United States has the right to intervene in other countries. In international politics, countries are recognized as independent, sovereign states.

These nations have the internationally recognized right to determine their own internal affairs, including their laws and systems of government. The United States has a long habit of taking an interest in other countries' politics, especially in the Western Hemisphere. It has done so even when other countries have disapproved or considered U.S. actions illegal.

In the nineteenth century and earlier, the United States generally avoided entering foreign conflicts. However, with the Spanish-American War of 1898, the United States began taking a more active role in the internal politics of other countries. Since then, the United States has used various methods to encourage a country to choose one leader over another. It has done so especially to encourage capitalist leaders over communist leaders. For example, the United States supported General Augusto Pinochet's seizure of power in Chile in 1973. Pinochet overturned the communist government of the previous president.

Carter's Visit

In 2002, Cuba received a distinguished visitor in Nobel Prize winner and former U.S. President Jimmy Carter. During a speech, Carter criticized the Cuban leadership for its human rights record but admitted that the death penalty was used more frequently in the United States than in Cuba. He also offered his view that the trade embargo should be lifted. Carter was the first former or current U.S. president to visit Cuba since Calvin Coolidge did so in 1928.

A Possible Security Risk

At the time sanctions were imposed on Cuba, the United States greatly feared the spread of communism around the world. Cuba was seen as the dangerous ally of the United States' enemy, the Soviet Union. The Cuban Missile Crisis reinforced this belief—the Soviets had placed missiles capable of reaching the United States on the island nation.

In addition, during the Cold War, Cuba itself often intervened in other countries. For example, in 1975, Cuba sent troops to support the African country of Angola during an invasion by its neighbor South Africa. Cuba also sent money and troops to aid political revolutionary movements in parts of Africa and Central America throughout the 1960s and 1970s.

Supporters of the sanctions argue that Cuba is a security risk—it poses a threat to the American way of life. Those who disagree say that Cuba is no longer actively supporting revolution around the world. It has not been economically or militarily capable or willing to become involved in other countries' affairs in recent years. Furthermore, they argue, no evidence shows that Cuba sponsors terrorism at home or around the world. Unlike countries such

Cuban women who belong to Ladies in White protested to demand the release of political prisoners in 2008.

as Iran and North Korea, Cuba has not threatened to create nuclear, biological, or chemical weapons. And though Castro and his fellow leaders have jailed political opponents, they have been outdone in this respect by leaders in China, a major U.S. trading partner.

However, supporters of sanctions argue that Cuba remains aggressive in spreading anti-U.S. feelings in Latin America. They also argue that Cuba has sold U.S. intelligence secrets to former and current enemies of the United States, such as Russia, China, North Korea, and Iran. In 2009, Cuba was one of four countries on the U.S. State Department's list of countries that sponsor terrorism. The State Department asserted that Cuba provided a safe haven for international terrorists and for U.S. fugitives.

Government Critic

Among the most outspoken critics of the Cuban government was Héctor Palacios Ruíz. He was the head of a dissident group called the Democratic Solidarity Party. He was arrested and sent to jail for 18 months for referring to Fidel Castro as "crazy" to a German television reporter.[1]

Ruíz was imprisoned a second time for his antigovernment activities in 2003. He was sentenced to 25 years but was released three years later. He eventually became a leader of an organization called Liberal Union, which works to bring democracy and a free-market system to Cuba.

Righting a Wrong

Some humanitarians may argue that sanctions are necessary in light of Cuba's terrible human rights record. Even if Cuba is a sovereign nation with the right to determine its own laws, the international community has standards for human rights that are reportedly not being met in Cuba. When these basic standards are not met, some argue, other countries have a duty to intervene for the sake of that country's residents. Humanitarians argue that the United States must take some action to try to improve human rights in Cuba. In their view, removing the sanctions would be a form of silent approval for Cuba's abuses.

Castro's government has taken away basic freedoms that are expected in other countries, including freedom of speech and the press, the freedom to assemble in groups, and the right to a trial. The government is controlled by one party. Elections may be held, but voters do not have a real choice in who represents them.

Varela Project

The Varela Project is a huge petition project in Cuba that has gathered thousands of signatures in support of Cuban democracy. The project is named for a nineteenth-century priest, Felix Varela. He worked to end slavery in Cuba and to bring about Cuban independence from Spain. The Varela Project is in accordance with the Cuban constitution, which allows for popular referendums. The citizens of Cuba can propose a law if at least 10,000 sign the petition.

In May 2002, the Varela Project gathered 11,020 signatures calling for fair elections, private businesses, freedom for political prisoners, and better human rights. Outside observers wondered if the Cuban government would allow this exercise of constitutional rights. Others argued that the Cuban constitution did not really allow for referendums of that type.

In June 2002, however, the Cuban government put together a referendum of its own. It allowed the government to change the constitution. The new Cuban constitution declared that the communist system could never be changed. The Varela Project continued, however, gathering 14,000 signatures in 2003 and launching another signature drive in fall 2008.

In 2008, the U.S. State Department reported that "the [Cuban] government continued to deny its citizens their basic human rights and committed numerous, serious abuses."[2] In 2008, the Cuban government held in prison at least 205 political dissidents. Other human rights organizations report that the Cuban government puts many more suspected political activists in jail for short amounts of time. These dissidents are not even told the crimes they are accused of. The Cuban government is also known to read the private communications of its citizens and to tightly control Internet access.

Supporters of sanctions argue that the United States cannot back down until the human rights abuses end. The U.S. government's position is to maintain the sanctions until Cuba releases political prisoners and allows its citizens more basic human rights.

Human Rights in China

China is governed by a single political party that has tight control over the speech, writings, assembly, and other basic rights of its people. It has a government-run media that bans any form of criticism. The occasional protest against the government in China has been stopped ruthlessly. In June 1989, a group of mostly student protesters were stopped by the Chinese military, leaving hundreds dead. In addition, China has been universally condemned for providing weapons and support for the government of Sudan, a country in northern Africa. War, disease, and famine have killed hundreds of thousands of people in the Darfur region of that country.

Comparing Cuba to China

The United States does not impose trade embargoes or travel restrictions on every communist country. China is also a communist state, and the United States has developed a working relationship with that Asian country. This difference might suggest that the sanctions against Cuba are based more on its human rights record than its form of government. However, China also has a poor human rights record, which includes a similar lack of freedom of speech and assembly.

Those who believe sanctions against Cuba are wrong point to the United States' far more open trade and travel policies with China. They contend that U.S. leaders are willing to ignore China's human rights record because of its importance in the global economy. The United States can bully Cuba because the latter has little power in the global economy, they say.

Critics of this opinion argue that political reality justifies the U.S. stance toward China. The Asian country plays a major role in the global economy and has a more powerful position on the global stage. Furthermore, China has lately seemed more open to capitalism. The United States is justified in encouraging these new capitalistic tendencies, critics argue.

Critics of the sanctions argue that China became more open to capitalism *because* the United States was willing to trade with it. They argue that lifting the sanctions would increase Cuban exposure to capitalism as well, which could encourage the Cuban people to bring an end to communism.

The military in China prevents its people from protesting.

Chapter 8

Americans protest the U.S. travel ban on Cuba.

Public Opinion

One can only speculate about what may happen between the United States and Cuba in the future. In the stormy world of politics, nothing ever stays the same. In relatively short spans, friends can become enemies, then friends once again. The same holds true for public opinion. While many U.S. leaders remained steadfast in their support of sanctions against Cuba, U.S. public opinion shifted against sanctions in the late 1990s. As of 2010, it stayed steady—more Americans were against sanctions than for them.

Americans and Cuban Americans

The views of Cuban Americans have always played a critical role in determining U.S. policy in Cuba. Until recent years, polls suggested that the majority of Cuban Americans favored sanctions as a means to force the Castro regime to make changes. But the new millennium brought a turn of the tide.

During his campaign, Barack Obama promised to find a new and friendlier path for Cuban-American relations. Following his election as U.S. president in 2008, a *Washington Post*/ABC News poll indicated that only 42 percent of Cuban Americans still backed the trade embargo. Though some organizations, such as Cuban Cultural Heritage, remain strongly in support of sanctions,

Cuban Americans

A huge majority of Cuban Americans live in Florida, especially in the southern part of the state. In fact, every community in the United States with a population consisting of 25 percent or more Cuban Americans is in Florida. Large pockets of Cuban immigrants are also found in California, Nevada, and New Jersey.

others have changed their position. The Cuban American National Foundation and the Cuba Study Group have supported President Obama's softened stance on Cuba. Younger Cuban Americans, in particular, have expressed a desire to see diplomatic and economic relations between the two countries.

According to a 1996 Gallup poll, 49 percent of U.S. voters supported sanctions on Cuba. But three years later, 71 percent *opposed* sanctions. At least 55 percent have maintained that opinion ever since. A 2009 Gallup poll claimed that 51 percent of Americans backed ending the trade embargo and that 64 percent favored ending travel restrictions.

People in the United States question if the current state of Cuban affairs deserves sanctions. They wonder if sanctions have brought Cuba any closer to democracy or if they will in the future. Most are now answering those questions with an emphatic no. President Obama has eased tensions by granting greater

Changing Opinions

Ricardo Herrero is a Cuban American who once supported the sanctions. In an interview with *Time* magazine, however, he explained why he changed his mind. "There are no better ambassadors of American culture and American democracy than Americans themselves."[1] He believes that ending the travel ban would lead to more contact between Cubans and Americans and that it would cause Cubans to want U.S. lifestyles for themselves.

President Barack Obama loosened some of the sanctions on Cuba.

visitation to Cuba and allowing Cuban Americans to send more money to relatives living on the island. Some hope that looser restrictions will help bring gradual change to the country.

Cubans and Democracy

How Cubans feel about democracy and capitalism has been shaped in part by the state-controlled media and ranges from total support to complete rejection. Kenia Serrano, a leader of the Union of Young Communists, expressed her view in the mid-1990s, and many of her peers feel the same way today. Serrano said:

> *If by democracy you mean homelessness, or you mean the democracy of racism, or where every four years parties organize a carnival and millions of dollars are spent, where candidates promise everything and nothing changes, then no, we don't want that kind of democracy.*[2]

Still, others are more optimistic about the possibility of democracy, and antigovernment activists and dissidents in Cuba continue to fight for it. Many of them have been jailed for expressing their political beliefs. One of the worst government crackdowns happened in March 2003. At that time, the Cuban government imprisoned 75 activists within days, including labor union leaders, librarians, and journalists. They became known as the "Group of 75."

Organizations including Ladies in White called for the release of these political prisoners and thousands of

Restrictions with Complications

Some U.S. legal experts assert that the recently loosened travel ban violates the constitutional rights of U.S. citizens. They declare that it is discriminatory to allow some groups of Americans travel privileges that are denied to other groups. The loosening also raises practical questions. Travelers cannot use their U.S. credit or debit cards in Cuba. U.S. travel agencies and insurance companies are not allowed to assist U.S. travelers with their Cuban visits, either. The 10 percent charge for converting dollars to convertible pesos also complicates matters.

others. Ladies in White is made up of women whose family members have been jailed for protesting. In advocating on behalf of political prisoners, they risked jail time themselves.

Advocating for democracy in Cuba does not necessarily mean supporting the U.S. sanctions, however. Oscar Espinosa Chepe, a dissident Cuban economist, represented the views of many when he wrote, "I have always been critical of the absurd U.S. policy of isolation and the embargo of Cuba."[3]

Some Cuban activists argue that Cubans must find their own solutions for their problems. As Mirriam Leiva, a member of Ladies in White, said:

Controversial Invitation

The Organization of American States (OAS) includes the nations of North and South America. The United States is the only OAS member that has imposed sanctions on Cuba. However, the group did suspend Cuba's membership in 1962. That changed in 2009 when the organization voted to revoke the measure. The OAS and U.S. officials stressed that Cuba's re-entry would not be immediate. The Castro regime would be forced to improve its human rights record and take steps toward democratization before an official invitation would be extended.

Among those who rallied against lifting the suspension was José Miguel Vivanco, the U.S. director of the organization Human Rights Watch. "OAS members have made an explicit commitment to promote human rights and the rule of law in the region," Vivanco said. "Ending Cuba's suspension would make a mockery of this pledge."[4] Cuba, however, had shunned the OAS, claiming that the organization is a puppet of the United States.

Only we Cubans, of our own volition . . . can decide issues of such singular importance. Cubans on the island have sufficient intellectual ability to tackle a difficult, peaceful transition and reconcile with other Cubans here and abroad.[5]

UN Vote

Cuba is a member state of the United Nations. In 2009, as the United Nations voted to censure the United States for its sanctions on Cuba, the Cuban representative spoke to the assembly. As reported by a journalist observer of the UN meeting, the representative "called the blockade an 'uncultured act of arrogance' that had hampered the development of Cuba's economy and was also applied to other countries that wanted to carry out business with the Caribbean nation. He said it was an 'absurd policy' that caused suffering and led to shortages of basic necessities. The embargo was a massive, flagrant and systematic violation of human rights."[6]

The World's Opinion

While the United States has held firm in its sanctions against Cuba, other countries have regularly expressed their disapproval. The United Nations' vote condemning the U.S. trade embargo against Cuba has become an annual event. The 185-to-3 landslide vote in 2009 marked the eighteenth consecutive year the UN General Assembly declared its disagreement with U.S. policy. It also marked the eighteenth consecutive year that the UN vote would be ignored.

The U.S. State Department's senior advisor for Latin American affairs, Ronald Godard, made a counterargument to the UN argument in 2007. In his view, the Cuban government should be condemned, not U.S. sanctions:

> *It is long past time that the Cuban people enjoy the blessings of economic and political freedom. . . . We urge member states to oppose and condemn the Cuban government's internal embargo on freedom, which is the real cause of the suffering of the Cuban people.*[7]

The European Union, a political and economic organization consisting of 27 nations, agreed to restore full diplomatic relations with Cuba in late 2008. An agreement with the island nation approved an immediate aid package of 2 million Euros (approximately $3 million) to rebuild areas damaged by Hurricanes Gustav and Ike. Approximately 36 million Euros ($53 million) more was made available to Cuba in 2009.

The Organization of American States (OAS) is an organization that fosters cooperation among the countries in North and South America. The OAS voted in June 2009 to permit Cuba to rejoin the group. The group continues to pressure Cuba to meet OAS standards for human rights and democracy. Although Cuban officials have stated that they have no intention of rejoining the OAS, this move has put more pressure on the U.S. government to return to normal relations with Cuba. Throughout 2009, the heads of several Latin American nations continued to pressure President Obama to work more quickly to ease or end restrictions and sanctions on Cuba.

The United States is mostly alone in its insistence on maintaining sanctions. Other countries object not only for moral reasons, but also because they do not believe that sanctions will ever motivate change in Cuba. In fact, most other countries believe that sanctions actually limit the spread of democracy. Exposure to democracy and capitalism through travel and a free-market system could inspire the Cuban people to demand change. Without the cooperation of the rest of the world, the United States' sanctions lose much of their effectiveness. Cuba is hurt less by the loss of U.S. trade when it is able to trade with most other countries.

The United Nations General Assembly votes every year to condemn the U.S. sanctions on Cuba.

Chapter 9

Since Raúl Castro's changes, some Cubans can buy goods that were unavailable in the country in the past.

The Present and the Future

Some aspects of Cuban life and government have been slowly changing in recent years. These changes have given some observers hope that the standoff between the United States and Cuba may soon come to an end. As Cuba and the United

States both make gradual changes, it seems possible that some common ground may be reached.

Raúl's Changes

Raúl Castro has softened some of Cuba's hard-line positions since taking over in 2008. He began allowing Cuban citizens to purchase items previously available to only foreigners and businesses, such as DVD players, computers, and microwaves. He also legalized the private use of cell phones. Raúl Castro also instituted political changes. Except for three people charged with terrorism, he reduced the sentences of Cubans who were to be put to death to jail time.

Meanwhile, the Cuban government reformed its pay rate structure for Cuban workers. It also increased pensions for the island country's 2 million retirees. Also, the state stopped dictating how much

Changing Attitudes

An indication that the Cuban government has softened its stand against those deemed political enemies occurred in 2009. Cuban physician Dr. Hilda Molina had tried in vain to obtain a visa to visit her son, grandchildren, and mother in Argentina. Doctors are often barred from leaving the country for nonmedical reasons because they are considered too valuable to the Cuban population. In addition, Molina had vocally disagreed with Castro on the ethics of some medical research.

In mid-June, however, the Cuban government granted her request. As Molina was about to board the plane, she broke down and cried. She had not seen her family in 15 years.

land farmers can use, what crops they can grow, and how much they can charge for their crops.

However, nothing indicates that the younger Castro brother will move toward democracy and capitalism in the near future. Most people believe that the changes made by Raúl were a response to practical needs in Cuba and have nothing to do with U.S. sanctions. Although Raúl has made several offers to meet with U.S. leaders, the United States will not meet with him unless Cuba improves its human rights record. Raúl has stated that he will negotiate with the United States only if:

> *they accept . . . our condition as a country that will not tolerate any blemishes on its independence, and as long as [the negotiation] is based on the principles of equality, reciprocity, non-interference, and mutual respect.*[1]

The United States' Best Interests

Some people wonder if U.S. leaders would end sanctions if they believed the United States would benefit financially. Some argue, for instance, that the critical issue of energy in this era of rising fuel costs could play a role. Cuba produces an estimated 53,000 barrels of oil a day and receives nearly another 90,000 barrels a day from Venezuela, its top trading partner. The two countries have partnered to build a major refinery in Cuba as well. Scientists estimate that Cuba has 4.6 billion barrels of oil reserves below the sea floor. If that figure is correct, Cuba could become the fourth-largest oil-producing nation in Latin America. Both the United States and Cuba would benefit from working together on oil exploration and production.

Tourism could be another income source for both countries if the travel ban were eliminated. Also, as of 2009, the United States provided the majority of Cuba's food and medical supplies. Opening trade could

Cuban Vacation

Tourism officials in Cuba and the United States are eagerly awaiting the day when the U.S. government lifts travel restrictions to the island. There is little doubt, however, that such a move would benefit Cuba far more than its northern neighbor. U.S. tourists have been flocking to Caribbean islands for many years, and curiosity alone would bring many of them to Cuba's sandy white beaches.

Tourism has grown into Cuba's top money producer, bringing the country approximately $2.5 billion a year. Cuba relies on tourists mostly from Canada and Europe. Cuba has several international airports to accommodate the estimated 2 million annual visitors.

The number of Americans receiving rare permission to visit Cuba every year numbers under 50,000. They generally represent universities, church groups, and media outlets, or they have been given visas to visit relatives. More Cuban Americans are expected to take advantage of President Obama's easing of travel restrictions for their group.

Cuban and American family members reunite. New rules make it easier for relatives from Cuba and the United States to visit.

increase U.S. business profits in these and other industries.

Some assert that, even if sanctions were lifted, the Cuban government would never allow a great deal of U.S. tourism and business. The majority of Cubans have spent their entire lives isolated under communist rule. Exposure to capitalism and democracy could motivate Cubans to take action against their own political and economic system. The prosanction faction believes the knowledge of that threat will prevent Cuban leaders from ever allowing much U.S. influence in their country.

What Has Not Worked

Those opposed to U.S. policy in Cuba stress the fact that sanctions have not worked. The point is difficult to argue. In 2009, Cuba was still committed to maintaining its communist system. Criticism of the government and its leaders was still strictly forbidden and treated severely. Many political opponents remained in Cuban jails.

Many feel that sanctions have backfired. They argue that attempting to isolate Cuba has served only to make the Castros sympathetic to their people and even to leaders of other nations. The U.S. sanctions help the Castros and the Cuban people appear as underdogs standing up to a bully. Fidel, in agreement with many Cubans, saw his country's resistance to sanctions as proof of their commitment to the revolution. As he explained in 2002 in response to tightened sanctions, "President Bush's pledge to maintain trade sanctions on Cuba was an 'insult' that 'multiplies the honor and glory of our people.'"[2]

People arguing against the sanctions say that the sanctions have not served to isolate Cuba. Though the United States has attempted over the years to persuade its allies to join the trade embargo and restrict travel, it has not been successful. Canada and the nations of Europe, though condemning Cuba for its human rights record and lack of freedom, have not joined the United States in punishing Cuba economically. In fact, Cuba is a frequent vacation destination for Canadians, and the rest of the world maintains normal diplomatic relations with Cuba. Cuba's allies and trading partners include China, Russia, and Venezuela. Many argue that sanctions imposed by just one country have no chance of being successful.

Can Change Come?

Many Americans hope that changes in Cuba will come from within. They point to events in Eastern Europe, where the people revolted against failed economies and repression. Uprisings in East Germany (1953), Hungary (1956), and Poland (1980) showed that people will rebel when they believe the government is unjust and ineffective. Eventually, their discontent helped end communism in the region. Many feel removing sanctions would expose Cubans to travelers who have experienced democracy, teach them about a free-market system, and motivate them to force change.

On the other hand, removing sanctions would return to Cubans the right to decide their own future. If the United States stopped trying to impose change, the Cuban people would be able to determine any changes for themselves—or to keep the system they have. Proponents of sanctions, however, argue that even if the sanctions were removed, the people would not have free choice because the Castros and the Communist Party would not allow it. Proponents argue that the purpose of U.S. pressure is to return power to the Cuban people so they can govern themselves.

New Changes

In April 2009, President Obama cleared the way for U.S. companies to bring U.S. cell phone and television networks to Cuba. The U.S. government no longer prohibits U.S. companies that provide these services from doing business in Cuba. It is hoped that giving Cubans greater access to the United States through such communication will advance the cause of freedom and democracy in Cuba.

Some claim that the United States is the only country in the world still fighting the Cold War and holding old grudges against Cuba. Others say that argument is an overstatement, given the relatively open relations the United States has developed with communist countries such as Vietnam and China. Some of those who back sanctions associate communism with a lack of freedom and basic human rights. They do not understand why U.S. allies such as Japan, Canada, Mexico, and the nations of Western Europe have not taken a similar stand against Cuba. However, critics believe that if U.S. officials justify sanctions by the lack of freedom in Cuba, they should stop U.S. companies from doing business with China as well.

In 2009, the new U.S. leadership showed a willingness to explore ways of bringing the United States and Cuba closer together by loosening the sanctions. And Raúl Castro has expressed his optimism that the Obama administration will be far more friendly to his country than the Bush one was.

Time inevitably brings change. Attitudes change. Policies change. However, no one can know for certain if Cuba will change enough to motivate the United States to remove sanctions or if the United States will decide to end sanctions on its own.

Former Communist State

Czechoslovakia is one former communist country whose leaders have been critical of their Cuban counterparts. Petr Kolar, the Czech ambassador to the United States, expressed his feelings in no uncertain terms: "The view of Czechs about Cubans is very positive. . . . I am very sorry that this gifted nation—those people who are really skilled and who can create wealth and provide welfare—are prevented from doing that by this crazy communist regime. . . . We know that we were cheated the whole time by our communist leaders and this is actually what [Fidel] Castro is doing."[3]

With time, Cuban and American relations may improve.

Timeline

1898

Cuba gains its independence from Spain when the United States wins the Spanish-American War.

1953

Fidel Castro and a band of 160 revolutionaries attack the barracks in Santiago de Cuba on July 26.

1958

Cuban president Fulgencio Batista resigns and flees the country on December 31.

1960

"Operation Pedro Pan," begins in November. It will transport 14,000 Cuban children to Florida.

1961

The Bay of Pigs invasion begins on April 15 but fails to overthrow the Castro government.

1962

The Soviet Union places nuclear missiles in Cuba in April.

1959	1960	1960
On January 2, Castro marches into Havana and declares the start of a new government.	On July 5, the Cuban government takes away all property owned by foreign countries.	The U.S. imposes an embargo on October 19 prohibiting all exports to Cuba except food and medical supplies.

1962	1980	1989
On October 14, the United States discovers the Soviet missiles. The nations come close to war during the Cuban Missile Crisis.	The Mariel Boatlift sends an estimated 125,000 people to the United States.	The end of the Soviet Union's aid to Cuba begins negatively affecting the Cuban economy. The Special Period begins.

Timeline

1992

The Cuban Democracy Act makes it more difficult for U.S. businesses to trade with Cuba.

1993

Cuba legalizes the use of U.S. dollars within its borders.

1996

Cuban planes shoot down two U.S. civilian planes on February 24.

2004

U.S. dollars are no longer accepted as currency in Cuba and must be exchanged for convertible pesos.

2006

Raúl Castro takes over leadership of Cuba on July 31 as brother Fidel falls ill.

2008

Fidel Castro hands over control of Cuba permanently to Raúl on February 19.

1996	1999	2002
The United States passes the Helms-Burton Act, which penalizes U.S. and foreign companies for doing business with Cuba.	Six-year-old Cuban refugee Elián Gonzalez is discovered on a life raft in the Straits of Florida in November.	Jimmy Carter becomes the first former or current U.S. president to visit Cuba since the Cuban Revolution.

2009	2009	2009
U.S. President Barack Obama eases travel restrictions to Cuba.	The Organization of American States votes to allow Cuba to rejoin the group; Cuba declines the invitation.	The United Nations votes for the eighteenth year in a row to condemn the U.S. sanctions on Cuba.

Essential Facts

At Issue

In Favor

- ❖ The United States should continue imposing sanctions to punish Cuba for its poor human rights record.
- ❖ Sanctions should be maintained to force Cuba to adopt a democratic form of government.
- ❖ Ending sanctions would help funnel funds into Cuba that would be used to strengthen the communist system. Sanctions are not the cause of Cuban poverty, the Cuban government is.

Opposed

- ❖ The majority of Americans, including Cuban Americans, are in favor of ending sanctions.
- ❖ The United States has established economic and diplomatic relations with countries that have worse human rights records than Cuba.
- ❖ It is not right for one country to impose sanctions in order to interfere in another country's internal affairs.
- ❖ The sanctions have not worked. U.S. trade and travel in Cuba would benefit both countries.
- ❖ The sanctions have caused more harm to the Cuban people than the Cuban government has caused.

Critical Dates

1959
Fidel Castro and fellow revolutionaries took over Cuba.

1960s
The United States and Cuba began a difficult relationship as the United States imposed sanctions on Cuba. The two countries had two major conflicts, the Bay of Pigs invasion in 1961 and the Cuban Missile Crisis in 1962.

1980s
The Mariel Boatlift brought more than 120,000 Cubans to the United States in 1980. In 1989, the loss of Soviet aid brought economic hardship to Cuba, and the Special Period began.

2000s
Many people began to hope for a change in U.S.-Cuban relations as Raúl Castro took over the Cuban government in 2008 and Barack Obama loosened some U.S. sanctions on Cuba in 2009. In 2010, most of the sanctions remained in place.

Quotes

"Concessions to the dictatorship [including ending the sanctions] embolden it to further isolate, imprison and brutalize pro-democracy activists, to continue to dictate which Cubans and Cuban-Americans are able to enter the island, and [provide] the dictatorship with critical financial support."—*U.S. Representatives Lincoln Diaz-Balart and Mario Diaz-Balart of Florida speaking against loosening the sanctions on Cuba, April 13, 2009*

"No democracy based on liberty should tell its citizens what country to visit or whom to trade with, regardless of the government under which they live. Even though the Castro brothers, Fidel and Raúl, would obtain a political victory in the very short run, the embargo could no longer be justified."—*Latin American expert Cuban Alvaro Vargas Llosa, April 2009*

Additional Resources

Select Bibliography

Erikson, Daniel P. *The Cuba Wars: Fidel Castro, the United States, and the Next Revolution*. New York, NY: Bloomsbury, 2008.

Galloway, George. *Fidel Castro*. London, UK: MQ Publications Ltd., 2006.

Gott, Richard. *Cuba: A New History*. New Haven, CT: Yale UP, 2004.

Sullivan, Mark P. "Cuba: Issues for the 111th Congress." *Congressional Research Service.* 14 Apr. 2009. 18 Nov. 2009 <www.fas.org/sgp/crs/row/R40193.pdf>.

Further Reading

Chrisp, Peter. *The Cuban Missile Crisis*. Milwaukee, WI: World Almanac Library, 2002.

Dunn, John M. *Life in Castro's Cuba*. San Diego, CA: Lucent Books, 2004.

Gay, Kathlyn. *Leaving Cuba: From Operation Pedro Pan to Elian*. Brookfield, CT: 21st Century Books, 2000.

Web Links

To learn more about U.S. sanctions on Cuba, visit ABDO Group online at **www.abdopublishing.com**. Web sites about U.S. sanctions on Cuba are featured on our Book Links page. These links are routinely monitored and updated to provide the most current information available.

For More Information

For more information on this subject, contact or visit the following organizations.

Cuban Art Space Gallery
231 West 29th Street, 4th Floor, New York, NY 10001
212-242-0559
www.cubanartspace.net/gallery/index.php
This museum features art, photographs, and posters created by Cuban artists.

Cuban Museum of Arts and Culture
1300 SW 12th Avenue, Miami, FL 33129
305-858-8006
This small museum of Cuban artists features traveling Cuban exhibitions every year.

Museum of Arts and Sciences: Cuban Foundation Museum
352 South Nova Road, Daytona Beach, FL 32114
386-255-0285
www.moas.org/Cuban%20Art.html
The museum holds one of the most important collections of Cuban art outside Cuba. The collection of more than 200 art objects documents three centuries of Cuban history.

Glossary

black market
A system by which goods are sold illegally.

capitalism
An economic system in which investments, businesses, and the production and distribution of wealth are controlled by private individuals or corporations, not the government.

Cold War
The period following World War II defined by tension between the United States and other democratic nations and communist countries such as the Soviet Union and China.

communism
A system in which social and economic activities are controlled by the government with the intention of an even distribution of wealth.

democracy
A form of government revolving around the power of the people to control their own lives, including freedom of speech and the election of leaders.

dictator
An individual who has absolute power in a country.

dissident
An individual who displays dissatisfaction with a government or its leaders.

doctrine
A belief of a group of people.

embargo
Any restriction of trade or other activity put in place by one government against another.

emigrate
To leave a home country and move to a new country.

exile
An individual who leaves a country voluntarily or is forced out, generally for political or philosophical reasons.

export
To send goods or services to another country for sale or exchange.

free market
The activity of buying and selling in a capitalist system.

humanitarian
A person who works to improve the lives of others.

immigrate
To come to live permanently in a new country.

import
To receive goods or services from another country for sale or exchange.

liberation
The act of gaining independence from control by another country.

referendum
A vote by all the people to change a law.

regime
The political party, leader, or government in power in a country.

repression
The act of controlling or denying the freedom of an individual or group of people.

revolutionary
An individual motivated to take action in an attempt to change or overthrow a government or its leadership.

sanctions
The policy of punishing another country through various means, such as by stopping trade or outlawing travel.

sovereign
Regarding a country, in control of one's own internal affairs.

terrorism
The use of violence or threats to gain political advantage.

visa
The documents a person needs to travel from one country to another.

Source Notes

Chapter 1. The Great Debate

1. Fidel Castro. "Message from the Commander in Chief." *www.cuba.cu.* 18 Feb. 2008. 16 Nov. 2009 <http://www.cuba.cu/gobierno/discursos/2008/ing/f180208i.html>.
2. Raúl Castro. "Key Address by Comrade Raúl Castro Ruz, President of the State Council and the Council of Ministers." *Juventude Rebelde*. 24 Feb. 2008. 16 Nov. 2009 <http://www.juventudrebelde.co.cu/cuba/2008-02-24/key-address-by-comrade-raul-castro-ruz-president-of-the-state-council-and-the-council-of-ministers/>.
3. Alvaro Vargas Llosa. "Free Trade: Should the U.S. Embargo on Cuba Finally Be Lifted?" *The New Republic*. 29 Apr. 2009. 2 June 2009 <http://www.tnr.com/article/politics/free-trade>.
4. "Diaz-Balart Brothers: Obama Commits Serious Mistake Regarding Cuban Dictatorship." *Naplesnews.com*. 13 Apr. 2009. 16 Nov. 2009 <http://www.naplesnews.com/news/2009/apr/13/diaz-balart-brothersobama-commits-serious-mistake-/>.

Chapter 2. Early History

1. Peter G. Bourne. *Fidel: A Biography of Fidel Castro*. New York, NY: Dodd, Mead, 1986. 1.
2. Castro Internet Archive. "History Will Absolve Me." *Marxists.org*. 2001. 27 May 2009. 10 Sept. 2009 <http://www.marxists.org/history/cuba/archive/castro/1953/10/16.htm>.

Chapter 3. Cold War History

1. "Fidel Castro's Trip to the United States: An Excerpt from the Book, *Family Portrait with Fidel* by Carlos Franqui, New York, NY: Random House, 1984." *HistoryofCuba.com*. 28 May 2009. 10 Sept. 2009 <http://www.historyofcuba.com/history/franqui3.htm>.
2. Tad Szulc. *Fidel: A Critical Portrait*. New York, NY: Harper, 2000. 482.
3. "Pedro Pan—'60s Evacuation of Cuban Kids Created Broken Families." *Chicago Tribune*. 12 Jan. 1998. 10 Sept. 2009 <http://www.cubanet.org/CNews/y98/jan98/13e5.htm>.

Chapter 4. Recent History

None.

Chapter 5. The Policy of Sanctions

1. Michael Paulson. "History of U.S. Sanctions Shows Most Haven't Worked." *Seattle Post-Intelligencer Online*. 11 May 1999. 3 Nov. 2009 <http://www.seattlepi.com/iraq/sanction.shtml>.
2. Jeremy Kinsman. "Cuban Transitions." *New York Times*. 22 Apr. 2009. 17 Nov. 2009 <http://www.nytimes.com/2009/04/23/opinion/23iht-edkinsman.html?adxnnl=1&adxnnlx=1258470061-rPANWWYeGPmGQ5AqYDu30w>.

Source Notes Continued

Chapter 6. The Castros and Life in Cuba

1. Raúl Castro. "Speech on the 50th Anniversary of the Revolution." *Juventude Rebelde*. 1 Jan. 2009. 17 Nov. 2009 <http://www.juventudrebelde.co.cu/cuba/2009-01-02/raul-castro-speech-on-the-50th-anniversary-of-the-revolution/>.
2. Rafael Rojas. "Fidel Castro's Feat." *American Experience: Fidel Castro*. 21 Dec. 2004. 17 Nov. 2009 <http://www.pbs.org/wgbh/amex/castro/sfeature/sf_views_rojas.html>.
3. Leycester Coltman. *The Real Fidel Castro*. New Haven, CT: Yale UP, 2003. 245.
4. George Galloway. *Fidel Castro*. London, UK: MQ Publications Ltd., 2006. 392.
5. Daniel P. Erikson. *The Cuba Wars: Fidel Castro, the United States, and the Next Revolution*. New York, NY: Bloomsbury, 2008. 237.

Chapter 7. The Right to Impose Sanctions

1. "Cuban Dissident Jailed for Calling Castro: 'Crazy.'" *Reuters*. 5 Sept. 1997. 10 Sept. 2009 <http://www.fiu.edu/~fcf/jailed.crazy9597.html>.
2. Bureau of Democracy, Human Rights, and Labor. "2008 Human Rights Report: Cuba." *U.S. Department of State*. 25 Feb. 2009. 17 Nov. 2009 <http://www.state.gov/g/drl/rls/hrrpt/2008/wha/119155.htm>.

Chapter 8. Public Opinion

1. Romina Ruiz-Goiriena. "Could the U.S.-Cuba Travel Ban End Soon?" *Time.* 4 Nov. 2009. 18 Nov. 2009 <http://www.time.com/time/world/article/0,8599,1934416,00.html?artId=1934416?contType=article?chn=world#ixzz0VzmaLqPy>.
2. Margarethe Siem. "'Human Beings Are the Most Important' Says Cuban Youth." *The Militant.* 11 Apr. 1995. 10 Sept. 2009 <http://www.hartford-hwp.com/archives/43b/016.html>.
3. Oscar Espinosa Chepe. "Black Spring of 2003: A Former Cuban Prisoner Speaks." *Committee to Protect Journalists Blog.* 17 Mar. 2009. 18 Nov. 2009 <http://cpj.org/blog/2009/03/the-black-spring-of-2003-a-former-cuban-prisoner-s.php>.
4. Human Rights Watch. "OAS: Maintain Suspension of Cuba." *HRW.org.* 1 June 2009. 10 Sept. 2009 <http://www.hrw.org/en/news/2009/06/01/oas-maintain-suspension-cuba>.
5. Mark P. Sullivan. "Cuba: Issues for the 111th Congress." *Congressional Research Service.* 20. 14 Apr. 2009. 18 Nov. 2009 <www.fas.org/sgp/crs/row/R40193.pdf>.
6. "Cuba: UN for the 18th Consecutive Year Demands End to U.S. Blockade." *United Nations.* 28 Oct. 2009. 18 Nov. 2009 <http://links.org.au/node/1324>.
7. "U.N. Again Urges U.S. to End Cuba Embargo." *CBS News Online.* 25 Oct. 2007. 1 Sept. 2009 <http://www.cbsnews.com/stories/2007/10/30/world/main3432040.shtml>.

Chapter 9. The Present and the Future

1. Mark P. Sullivan. "Cuba: Issues for the 111th Congress." *Congressional Research Service*. 21. 14 Apr. 2009. 18 Nov. 2009 <www.fas.org/sgp/crs/row/R40193.pdf>.
2. "Case Studies in Sanctions and Terrorism." *Peterson Institute for International Economics*. 18 Nov. 2009 <http://www.iie.com/research/topics/sanctions/cuba2.cfm>.
3. Daniel P. Erikson. *The Cuba Wars: Fidel Castro, the United States, and the Next Revolution*. New York, NY: Bloomsbury, 2008. 299.

Index

About the Author

Martin Gitlin was a reporter for two newspapers in northeast Ohio for 20 years before becoming solely a freelance writer. During his two decades as a reporter, Gitlin won more than 40 awards, including first place for general excellence from the Associated Press in 1995. The Associated Press also named him one of the top four features writers in the state of Ohio in 2001. Gitlin has written approximately 20 books about sports and history.

Photo Credits

José Luis Samayoa/Photolibrary, cover, 3; Red Line Editorial, 6; AP Images, 8, 17, 23, 24, 27, 30, 42, 62, 96, 97 (top), 97 (bottom), 98 (top); Ricardo Mazalan/AP Images, 13; North Wind Picture Archives/Photolibrary, 14; Andrew St. George/AP Images, 20; Jacques Langevin/AP Images, 35; Alejandro Balguer/AP Images, 36; Javier Galeano/AP Images, 45, 69, 86, 98 (bottom); Mark Wilson/AP Images, 46; Bill Bachmann/Photolibrary, 48; Angelo Cavalli/Photolibrary, 55; Cristobal Herrera/AP Images, 56; Jose Goitia/AP Images, 65; Naeem Khan/AP Images, 66; Kyodo/AP Images, 75; Don Heupel/AP Images, 76; Matt Rourke/AP Images, 79, 99; Mary Altaffer/AP Images, 85; J. Pat Carter/AP Images, 90; Lynne Sladky/AP Images, 95